FROM STRESSED TO BLESSED

GOD'S INSPIRING WORDS THROUGH PSALMS...

Victoria Grace

Copyright © 2024 *Victoria Grace*

All rights reserved.

Dedication

I dedicate this book to my dear husband Joe, and my two daughters, Davina and Danica.

Most importantly, I dedicate this book to our Lord and Savior Jesus Christ.

Acknowledgments

I want to acknowledge my wonderful husband who is a constant encouragement to me. He helps me believe in myself and do what God has intended for me to do. My thanks to God and to my husband.

About the Author

Victoria Grace is a dedicated and faithful servant of the Lord Jesus Christ, Sunday school teacher (children and adults), Homegroup Leader, Life Coach, Christian Motivational Speaker, author, educator and Ladies Group Facilitator. My experience in social services for twenty years has given me different perspectives in life and the world. In my free time, I like spending my time outdoors as I enjoy nature and photography which is my hobby. My writing derives from my everyday life experiences and is inspired by reading the words of God (Bible) everyday.

Through Jesus Christ who gives me strength, I am able to face the reality of my past, lay everything down at the feet of Jesus. To forgive myself as the Lord has forgiven me. Through all my life's experiences God is always there with me, loving me as it says in Jeremiah 29:11 "For I know the plans I have for you," declares the Lord, "plans to prosper you and not to harm you, plans to give you hope and a future."

PREFACE

To develop an attitude of gratitude; we need to express our gratefulness and be thankful for everything and for everyone. It should continue as a part of our lives, in every area of our lives. Psalms is a book in the Bible filled with thanksgiving and praise.

1 It is a good thing to give thanks unto the LORD, and to sing praises unto thy name, O most High:

2 To shew forth thy lovingkindness in the morning, and thy faithfulness every night,

~Psalm 92:1-2

Thank those who help you.

7 And he took him by the right hand and lifted him up: and immediately his feet and ankle bones received strength.

8 And he leaping up stood, and walked, and entered with them into the temple, walking, and leaping, and praising God.

9 And all the people saw him walking and praising God:

10 And they knew that it was he which sat for alms at the Beautiful gate of the temple: and they were filled with wonder and amazement at that which had happened unto him.

~Acts 3:7-10

Thank those who brought you joy.

For what thanks can we render to God again for you, for all the joy wherewith we joy for your sakes before our God;) Give thanks in everything. Our joy, prayers and thankfulness should not fluctuate with our situation. It doesn't mean we should give thanks FOR everything but IN everything.

~1 Thessalonians 3:9

In everything give thanks: for this is the will of God in Christ Jesus concerning you.

~1 Thessalonians 5:18

When we do God's will, we will find it easier to be joyful and thankful.

> ***Great is the LORD, and greatly to be praised in the city of our God, in the mountain of his holiness.***
>
> ***~Psalm 48:1***

The beauty and the mighty works of God our Father!
Thunder and lightning are awe-inspiring.
The moon and the stars are perfectly placed in the sky.
The birds are sweetly singing Hallelujah.
The trees, with their luscious leaves, gently swaying with the wind.
The flowers in the meadow bring out the color of love and the aroma of life.
The vastness and the depth of the ocean no one can measure.
The heights of the mountains and the valleys below.
I am in constant awe of the wonders of your work, O LORD!
Truly, O LORD my God, how great is your art.
My heart sings your praises with thankfulness.
O LORD my Lord, how excellent is your name in all the earth!
I am blessed beyond measure. Thank you, Lord God Almighty!!!

Rejoice in the Lord and be glad, you righteous; sing, all you who are upright in heart!

~Psalm 32:11

To rejoice in the Lord always is to thank and to give all glory to God in good times and in bad times. When our hearts are right with God we can sing for joy always. We sometimes feel as though there is no hope when the going is tough. Let us remember that God is in control of everything. Rejoice always and be glad that we are given another day, another chance to glorify God and sing for joy.

> ***One thing I ask of the LORD, this is what I seek: that I may dwell in the house of the LORD all the days of my life, to gaze upon the beauty of the LORD and to seek him in his temple.***
>
> ***~Psalm 27:4***

We often run to God when we face difficulties instead of seeking God every day. God is our light, and we delight in His presence always. Often, our pride deters us from building a wonderful relationship with God. I pray that we spend time with God and gaze upon His beautiful face always. May we love God and dwell in the house of the Lord forever and ever. Amen.

Blessed is the one whose transgressions are forgiven, whose sins are covered. 2 Blessed is the one whose sin the Lord does not count against them and in whose spirit is no deceit.

~Psalm 32:1-2

Forgiveness has always been part of God's loving nature. God wants to forgive sinners, and he announces through Jesus Christ. God's forgiveness - pointing us to the light. The joy of being forgiven and the experience of forgiveness come through faith in Jesus Christ. When God forgive our sins, he counts it no more. How wonderful it is to be forgiven by God our Lord Jesus Christ.

1 God is our refuge and strength an ever-present help in trouble.

2 Therefore we will not fear, though the earth give way and the mountains fall into the heart of the sea,

3 though its waters roar and foam and the mountains quake with their surging.

~Psalms 46:1-3

We fear that the mountains and cities crumbling into the sea by a nuclear blast and terrorists haunt us today. However, God assures us that even to the world's ends, we need not fear. Let us express a quiet confidence in God that can save us even in the face of utter destruction. God is not merely a temporary refuge, but he is our eternal refuge. God gives us the strength to face the uncertainties of life. Trust him fully.

> ***Whom have I in heaven but You? And besides You, I desire nothing on earth. My flesh and my heart may fail, But God is the strength of my heart and my portion forever.***
>
> ***~Psalms 73:25-26***

God is the source of our daily needs and life itself. He wants us to understand the importance of giving Him glory and honor. There is nothing in this world that can fulfill our needs. Hence, we have nothing to worry about whether we are rich or poor, weak or strong, because God loves us just the same. Look at our life through heaven's eyes. Let us worship God in all that we do and wherever we go.

***Though the Lord is exalted, he looks kindly on the lowly;
though lofty, he sees them from afar.***

~Psalm 138:6

As we watch from a distance as to what is happening in our community and the world, it is hard to fathom and understand the pains and sufferings these people are going through. No one is immune to pain and suffering. Let's continually pray that during calamity, people around the world will find God's love and peace.

Not to us, Lord, not to us but to your name be the glory, because of your love and faithfulness.

~Psalm 115:1

God's name alone is glorified. Too often, we ask God to glorify his name with ours. We pray for help to do a good job, so that our work will be noticed. There is nothing wrong with looking good or impressing others. If our glory is a by-product of seeking God's glory, seek God first always and give him all the glory.

***3 Lord, what are human beings that you care for them,
mere mortals that you think of them?***

***4 They are like a breath; their days are like a fleeting
shadow.***

~Psalms 144:3-4

Let us live for God. He alone can make our lives worthwhile, purposeful, and meaningful.

Life is short, and we are but a breath, dust in the wind, and our days are like passing shadows. The days of our lives are uncertain and unpredictable. Let us not waste our lives. Because life is short, we should live it for God while we have time.

> **7Answer me quickly, Lord;my spirit fails. Do not hide your face from me or I will be like those who go down to the pit.**
>
> **8 Let the morning bring me word of your unfailing love, for I have put my trust in you. Show me the way I should go,for to you I entrust my life.**
>
> **~Psalm 143:7-8**

There are moments in our lives when we lose hope, as we are caught in a deep depression that seems to paralyze us with fear so deep that we are unable to pull ourselves out. During this time, we can come to the Lord. God will help us as we remember his miracles. Trust God always, especially during the darkest hour of our lives. Let trust and faith affect our lives' perspectives and give us the strength to face uncertain days.

Blessings on all who reverence and trust the Lord---on all who obey Him. Their reward shall be prosperity and happiness.

~Psalms 128:1 - 2

May we find ways to be in constant obedience to God's leading our lives. We are but mere human beings, humbled by the grace and mercy of God. God loves us in spite of and regardless of what we have done. When we trust and obey, we learn that there is no other way but to trust and obey. May the Lord continually bless you with heaven's blessings as well as human joys.

***3 Do not put your trust in princes, in human beings,
who cannot save.***

***4 When their spirit departs, they return to the ground;
on that very day their plans come to nothing.***

***5 Blessed are those whose help is the God of Jacob,
whose hope is in the Lord their God.***

~Psalm 146: 3-5

Let us put our trust in God alone. God's provisions never end; sometimes, we put our trust in others, and they let us down and sometimes hurt us. The Lord will stand by us and ultimately bring about justice. This should be a comfort to all of us. No matter what we do or where we go, we can never be far from God's comforting presence.

Those who trust in the Lord are as steady as the Mount Zion, unmoved by any circumstance.

~Psalms 125:1

Don't be discouraged. No circumstance is ever difficult when we trust in the Lord. In time of our need God is on our side. God will provide a way out. We need only to trust him. God never changes and will keep us steady and secure. Whatever circumstances we are in, it is part of God's grand design. God is sovereign in every area of our lives. With God in charge, we can take the courage. God guides us through the circumstances we face in our lives. God will display his power in carrying out his will. As we unite our life's purpose to God's purpose we benefit from his sovereign care.

Let everything alive give praises to the Lord... Praise Him.

~Psalms 150:6

Godly people still face both blessings and troubles, joy and grief, successes and obstacles. Throughout it all, God is at our side, guiding, encouraging, comforting, and caring. Praising God during the storm is the hardest thing to do. Praising God for His leadership and for the assurance He gives us upon entering His perfect world, God has blessings in store for those who have faithfully followed Him.

For all God's words are right, and everything he does are worthy of our trust.

~Psalms 33:4

All of God's words are true and trustworthy. We can trust God because he is unchanging, and He fulfills his promise to all mankind. If we trust God, it is because we trust that He is God who claims to be Almighty. When we doubt God and His words, then we doubt the integrity of God Himself. Believe that God is truly God and believe everything He says.

Lord you have examined my heart and know everything about me. When far away, you know my thoughts. You chart the path ahead of me; you tell me where to stop and rest. Every moment you know where I am. You precede and follow me, and place your hand of blessing upon me.

~Psalms 139:1-5

God knows everything about us, but He loves us. Nonetheless, God is always with us through every situation and every trial - protecting, loving, and guiding us. However, we don't let people know us completely because we are afraid they will discover something about us they won't like. It's alright not to let everyone know about us... But God knows us completely.

> ***God is our refuge and strength, an ever-present help in trouble. Therefore, we will not fear, though the earth gives way and the mountains fall into the heart of the sea, though its waters roar and foam and the mountains quake with their surging.***
>
> ***~Psalm 46:1-3***

We all feel fear and often feel defeated. God's ability to save us from all troubles, even in the face of utter destruction, is unfathomable. God is an everlasting refuge, not just a temporary retreat. Whenever we feel that fear is starting to cripple us and doubts are setting in, we look to God and give to Him all our troubles and worries. God loves and protects those who love Him. Let God be God because He is God, and we are not.

We often ask what the world is coming to; with all these changes happening around us We often ask where God in all of these is. God never leaves us, but He allows things to happen for us to learn what is right and what is wrong. We say the world is corrupt, but we are part of this world. As Christians and followers of Jesus Christ, we need not to look at the world in worldly passion but look at the world through heaven's eyes. With strong faith and with God's love - we can love the unlovable. After all, who are we to judge one another? We will miss God's presence and calling when we are focused on ourselves, what is going on around us, and what is good for us alone by disregarding what is more important. Love God and love others is God's greatest commandments to all. Love regardless. We all fall short, and we all live an imperfect life.

1 We live within the shadow of the Almighty, sheltered by the God who is above all gods.

2 This I declare, that He alone is my refuge, my place of safety; he is my God, and I am trusting him.

~Psalms 91:1-2

I believe that whether I live or die, I belong to my Lord and Savior, Jesus Christ. Death is merely seeing the Lord face to face. If we are not ready to die, then we are not ready to live.

When we realize that life is short, it helps us use the little time we have more wisely. We concentrate on using our lives for eternal good, not just for the pleasure of the moment. It may look like we are surrounded by enemies (evil), but the Lord surrounds us with love and protection.

These things I have spoken to you, that in Me you may have peace. In the world, you will have tribulation, but be of good cheer, I have overcome the world.

~John 16:33

Take time to number your days by asking, "What do I want to see happen in my life before I die?"

Deteremine what small step could you take toward that purpose today.

I will praise the LORD, who counsels me; even at night my heart instructs me.

~Psalm 16:7

It is human nature that we make our own plans and then ask God to bless them. Instead, we should seek God's will first. By constantly thinking about the Lord and his way of living, we will gain insight that will help us make the right decisions and live the way God desires us to live our lives.

I called on the Lord in distress; The Lord answered me and set me in a broad place. The Lord is on my side; I will not fear. What can man do to me?

~Psalm 118:5-6

Trust God always in every circumstance, as He is always on our side. Let us put our full confidence in God, and He will guide us here on earth towards our eternal destination. God is with us always no one can harm us.

Yet I am confident I will see the Lord's goodness while I am here in the land of the living.

~Psalm 27:13

It doesn't matter what our circumstances are now. Think positive, expect favorable results and situations, and circumstances will change accordingly. Positive thinking is a mental attitude. A positive mind anticipates happiness, joy, health, and a successful result. Let God transform and renew our way of thinking daily.

> *I will remember the deeds of the Lord; yes, I will remember your miracles of long ago. I will consider all your works and meditate on all your mighty deeds.*
>
> *~Psalms 77:11-12*

Memories of God's goodness and faithfulness sustain us through our difficulties and during our trials and tribulations. We know God is able and He is trustworthy. When we have new trials, let us review the good things that God has done in our lives, and this will strengthen our faith. We have everything we need. All we must do is believe. Miracles still happen every day.

Give thanks to the God of heaven, for his steadfast love endures forever.

~Psalm 136:26

Are we struggling with an area of our life today and looking for peace, acceptance, and love?

There are moments when we feel far away from God's loving hands. Somehow, God finds ways to draw us nearer to Him. We can see God anywhere and everywhere if we love and obey Him. God's amazing love and grace are truly hard to fathom.

Answer me when I call to you, my righteous God. Give me relief from my distress; have mercy on me and hear my prayer.

~Psalm 4:1

Nothing is hidden from God - this can be either comforting or terrifying. God knows our motives, and nothing is hidden from him. The very knowledge that we cannot hide anything from God is comforting. Our thoughts are open book to Him. God knows our thoughts. We do not need to impress Him or pretend or put up a front for Him. Instead, we can trust God to help us work through our weaknesses. God will restore our spirit, and we will be lifted.

You made me; you created me. Now give me the sense to follow your commands.

~Psalm 119:73

COME WHAT MAY

Disappointments often beset us... come what may. Sometimes, we bring disappointment unto ourselves. Having unrealistic expectations from ourselves and others. Our actions or spoken words may result in breaking up of a beautiful friendship/relationship. Often our carelessness can cause a falling out on a steady situation.

Promises we make to ourselves and to others are often just words without action. We all experience disappointments, and we also disappoint others, either intentionally or unintentionally. Come what may...Live and let live, as life is a journey in which the road is not always smooth. Life is a classroom where we are constantly learning and discovering about ourselves and others. Expect less from ourselves and others, and strive for the best. Let our expectations be for the benefit of all mankind. May we find peace in all that we do. Come what may...May God shine His beautiful face upon us always...

Even perfection has its limits, but your commands have no limit. Oh, how I love your instructions! I think about them all day long.

~Psalm 119:96-97

The world is full of evil and cruelty. How can God's word revive us? God's word gives us assurance and value as He loves us. As we obey God's commands, we gain knowledge and wisdom of his lovingkindness. God renews our hearts and minds. God promises victory over evil. Our world is full of discouragements, but God encourages us. The world does not give us real answers about life; God's word is eternal, and it gives us satisfying answers. God's word teaches us to make a difference in our lives and others.

Do not let my heart be drawn to what is evil so that I take part in wicked deeds along with those who are evildoers; do not let me eat their delicacies.

~Psalms 141:4

Temptations are always around us. Thus, we need to pray that God changes our hearts' desires. Evil acts begin with evil desires. Ask God to take away our lustful and envious desires. Let God transform our hearts and renew our minds.

You have made my days a mere handbreadth; the span of my years is as nothing before you. Everyone is but a breath, even those who seem secure.

~Psalms 39:5

Waiting for God to help us is not easy. Only a few people understand that our only hope is in the Lord. Ironically, we spend a lot of time acquiring wealth and earthly possessions, and we spend little time or no thought about where we will spend eternity. We realize quite late in life that amassing earthly riches and busily accomplishing tasks would make no difference in eternity.

As the deer pants for streams of water, so my soul pants for you, my God.

~Psalms 42:1

There are moments in our lives when we thirst for God. We weep in sorrow, and we are ridiculed. God remains silent. Such times lead to depression and discouragement. Remember God's great blessings in our lives. Although we feel insurmountable sorrow, God is there to receive our praises. When God seems so far away, do not be dismayed. We are never adrift from God's steadfast love.

There are several advantages of having faith in God. God guards the minds and actions of those who follow His commands. Blessings overflow to those who abide by the Lord.

1 Praise the Lord. Blessed are those who fear the Lord, who find great delight in his commands.

2 Their children will be mighty in the land; the generation of the upright will be blessed.

3 Wealth and riches are in their houses, and their righteousness endures forever.

4 Even in darkness light dawns for the upright, for those who are gracious and compassionate and righteous.

5 Good will come to those who are generous and lend freely, who conduct their affairs with justice.

6 Surely the righteous will never be shaken; they will be remembered forever.

7 They will have no fear of bad news; their hearts are steadfast, trusting in the Lord.

8 Their hearts are secure; they will have no fear; in the end they will look in triumph on their foes.

9 They have freely scattered their gifts to the poor, their righteousness endures forever; their horn will be lifted high in honor.

10 The wicked will see and be vexed, they will gnash their teeth and waste away;the longings of the wicked will come to nothing.

~Psalms 112

Many blessings are available to us – honor, prosperity, security, freedom from fear – if we fear the Lord. Trust in Him and delight in obeying His commands. When we expect God's blessings, we must first revere Him, believe in His promises, and gladly obey His commands.

We all want to live without fear. The Psalms teach us that fear of God can lead to a fearless life. When we trust God completely to take care of us, we will find that our other fears will completely diminish, even the fear of death. Therefore, living our life for the Lord is a blessing in itself.

His concern demonstrates God's great mercy for the poor and the oppressed.

> *1 Praise the LORD. Praise the LORD, you his servants;*
> *praise the name of the LORD.*
>
> *2 Let the name of the LORD be praised, both now and forevermore.*
>
> *3 From the rising of the sun to the place where it sets, the name of the LORD is to be praised.*
>
> *4 The LORD is exalted over all the nations, his glory above the heavens.*
>
> *5 Who is like the LORD our God, the One who sits enthroned on high,*
>
> *6 who stoops down to look on the heavens and the earth?*
>
> *7 He raises the poor from the dust and lifts the needy from the ash heap;*
>
> *8 he seats them with princes, with the princes of his people.*

9 He settles the childless woman in her home as a happy mother of children. Praise the LORD.

~Psalms 113

In God's eyes, our value has no relationship to our wealth or position on the social ladder. Many people who have excelled in God's work began in poverty or humble beginnings. God supersedes the social order of this world. In God's eyes, we are all equal. No one is poor or rich.

Today, we put more value on tangible objects (money, position, home, clothing, possessions) than on intangible objects (spiritual growth, salvation, giving to those in need, spending time with our loved ones). Those who give time to these tangible objects are as foolish and empty as the idols themselves.

15 When he calls on me, I will answer; I will be with him in trouble and rescue him and honour him.

16 I will satisfy him with a full life and give him my salvation.

~Psalms 91:15 -16

As Christians with sensible minds and thinking, we need to stop letting uncertainty put fear in our lives. There are so many diseases that are contagious and potentially fatal, but we don't stop living our lives. I refuse to let anything stop me from living my life as normally as possible. We let fear engulf us, and Satan uses fear to defeat us. For Christians who truly trust the Lord Jesus Christ it is time for us to rise and stand up, let our voice of truth be heard.

It is saints' time to march and claim our freedom to worship our Lord and Savior, Jesus Christ. Fear has no hold on those who follow our Lord. I am not saying to put our lives in danger deliberately. Read your Bible. You'll find the Lord's protection and assurance that God will protect us from all harms, dangers, and snares. Put on the full armor of God as our battle against darkness has just begun. Lies and deceptions are shaping the minds of those with evil intentions. Trust in the Lord and lean not on your own understanding. In all your ways, acknowledge our Lord Jesus Christ, and he will direct you to the path of righteousness.

Don't Put Your Leaders On A Pedestal

Put not your trust in princes, nor in the son of man, In whom there is no help.

~Psalms 146:3

Some kings, leaders and nations often think that they are unbeatable and untouchable; they become arrogant and egotistical. They are proud of themselves and forget about their Maker, our Lord Jesus Christ.

The longer a person stays in power, the more likely that leader will become unreasonable, unjust, and unmerciful. The pride and arrogance will increase.

Woe to those who enact evil statutes. And to those who constantly record unjust decisions.

~Isaiah 10:1

God will judge the crooked leaders and those who make unfair laws. Those who oppress others will be oppressed themselves. You are accountable to God for what you do. Godless leaders will be doomed. We need to pray for our leaders that the Lord will grant them godly wisdom and rule the nation in a godly manner where God reigns in their midst.

Like a roaring lion and a rushing bear. Is a wicked ruler over a poor people.

~Proverbs 28:15

A lawless nation will have many bad leaders. A leader who takes advantage of the poor. Those who refuse to obey the law promote evil. The wicked don't understand justice.

When the righteous increase who, the people rejoice, but when a wicked man rules, people groan.

~Proverbs 29:2

Calamity will come upon the wicked leaders on the day of the Lord.

To be a wise leader, you need to be open to others' counsel and advice. Do not be blinded by bias, wrong impressions, or emotions. A good leader uses wise counsellors as one person's perspective is limited. If our world leaders seek guidance from God, our Creator, we may not have war, famine, or injustice; seek guidance from the Lord. After considering all the facts, make your decision as the Lord leads you.

Jesus Christ's Kingdom will replace and surpass the kingdoms of the world. Our faith is sure because our future is secure in Jesus Christ. Amid persecution, we must have courage and put our faith in God, who controls everything.

Make me to go in the path of thy commandments; for therein do I delight.

~Psalms 119:35

I have so much to be thankful for. The Lord places me where He is needed, in His time. Some people ask me how I spend my time. Simple, really, I serve anywhere and everywhere the opportunity arises. To see that the Lord is at work in people's lives I encountered and leave them better than when I met them is a blessing in itself.

God changed my position to change my perspective. I moved, my job changed as did places I have held in people's hearts. Each change brings another opportunity for God to change my perspective. Like the disciples, I can see JESUS CHRIST in new ways I haven't seen Him before, my Provider, my Healer, my Light and Salvation, my True Love. My Lord and my Savior Jesus Christ.

When we live our lives according to God's will, we see the goodness of God around us. To lead one lost soul to Jesus Christ, Heaven celebrates.

> ***I will praise the name of God with a song and will magnify him with thanksgiving. This also shall please the LORD better than an ox or bullock that hath horns and hoofs. The humble shall see this, and be glad: and your heart shall live that seek God.***
>
> ***~Psalms 69:30-32***

When we focus on trying to please God with our tithes alone, we may be forgetting that He wants to hear us praise Him and thank Him. While Cain gave God an offering, his brother Abel's offering from his heart was more pleasing to God. When we honor God with our words and hearts, we show that God does not love those with more wealth more than those who are poor. He loves our hearts.

The Lord does not love like the world loves. God loves us with everlasting love, and the Lord deserves our praise and thanksgiving. Remember that our offerings reflect our hearts. The Lord cares more about our hearts than the offerings that we can afford. May we live a life of thanksgiving that brings God the glory and shows others God's goodness.

David cried out to God when he was in depths of despair. God heard his cry, and he comforted him.

1 Deliver me from my enemies, O God; be my fortress against those who are attacking me.

2 Deliver me from evildoers and save me from those who are after my blood.

3 See how they lie in wait for me! Fierce men conspire against me for no offense or sin of mine, Lord.

4 I have done no wrong, yet they are ready to attack me. Arise to help me; look on my plight!

5 You, Lord God Almighty, you who are the God of Israel, rouse yourself to punish all the nations; show no mercy to wicked traitors.

6 They return at evening, snarling like dogs, and prowl about the city.

7 See what they spew from their mouths—the words from their lips are sharp as swords, and they think, "Who can hear us?"

8 But you laugh at them, Lord; you scoff at all those nations.

9 You are my strength, I watch for you; you, God, are my fortress,

10 my God on whom I can rely. God will go before me and will let me gloat over those who slander me.

11 But do not kill them, Lord our shield, or my people will forget. In your might uproot them and bring them down.

12 For the sins of their mouths, for the words of their lips, let them be caught in their pride. For the curses and lies they utter,

13 consume them in your wrath, consume them till they are no more. Then it will be known to the ends of the earth that God rules over Jacob.

14 They return at evening, snarling like dogs, and prowl about the city.

15 They wander about for food and howl if not satisfied.

16 But I will sing of your strength, in the morning I will sing of your love; for you are my fortress, my refuge in times of trouble.

17 You are my strength, I sing praise to you; you, God, are my fortress, my God on whom I can rely.

~Psalms 59

We live in a world where unfairness and injustice seem to triumph. The rich get richer, and the poor get poorer. When wrong seems right, and the darkness hovers us relentlessly. Standing up for what is right is a fight we battle each day. Giving up is sometimes the best, and succumbing to the lure of unrighteousness.

Our eyes become a fountain of tears. Our hearts are heavily burdened with sadness and sorrow. Through it all, we will discover God's everlasting love. God also comforts us during our struggles and distress. Stand firm and trust in the Lord, God Almighty.

19 Many are the afflictions of the righteous, but the LORD delivers him out of them all.

20 he protects all his bones, not one of them will be broken.

~Psalms 34:19-20

Afflictions - trouble, difficulties, and disappointments - occur in a sinful world. How you look at your troubles makes all the difference in the world! Do you think about them, talk about them, focus on them, and imagine a few extra? Do you let the devil drag your spirit down to the hell of depression and a defeated life?

Let God be the center of our focus, the center of our lives, so that there will be no room for such things.

Cast your burden on the Lord, and he will sustain you; he will never permit the righteous to be moved.

~Psalms 55:22

Do not be discouraged. No circumstance is ever difficult when we trust in the Lord. In time of our need God is on our side. God will provide a way out. We need only to trust him. God never changes and will keep us steady and secure. The Lord said to place our worries onto Him so that he may shoulder our burdens for us. There is no need for us to face our struggles alone.

One theme in the poetic literature of the Bible is that God is incomprehensible. We can not know Him completely. But we can gain knowledge about Him. The Bible is full of details about who God is; how we can know Him, and we can have an eternal relationship with Him.

We can never know enough to answer all of life's questions (Ecclesiastes 3:11), to predict our own future, or to manipulate God for our own ends. Life always has more questions than answers, and we must constantly go to God for fresh insights into life's dilemmas through Christ Jesus.

In closing, if you haven't accepted Jesus Christ as your Lord and Savior, pray this simple prayer.

A Simple Sinner's Prayer

For all have sinned and fall short of the glory of God.

~Romans 3:23

Dear Heavenly Father, I come to you in the name of Jesus Christ. I acknowledge to You that I am a sinner, and I am sorry for my sins and the life that I have lived; I need Your forgiveness.

For God so loved the world that he gave his one and only Son, that whoever believes in him shall not perish but have eternal life.

~John 3:16

I believe that your only Son, Jesus Christ, shed His precious blood on the cross at Calvary and died for my sins, and I am now willing to repent, confess, and turn from my sins. You said in the Bible that if I confess to the Lord our God and believe in my heart that God raised Jesus from the dead, I shall be saved.

Jesus answered, "I am the way and the truth and the life. No one comes to the Father except through me.

~John 14:6

I confess Jesus Christ as my Lord and my Savior. With my heart, I believe that God raised Jesus from the dead. This very moment, I accept Jesus Christ as my own personal Savior, and according to His Word, right now I am saved. Amen.

www.ingramcontent.com/pod-product-compliance
Lightning Source LLC
Chambersburg PA
CBHW051317110526
44590CB00031B/4381